JAZZ IN PERSPECTIVE

JAZZ
IN PERSPECTIVE

BY CHARLES FOX

THE BRITISH BROADCASTING CORPORATION

The Programmes

Details of the BBC radio programmes
which this book accompanies:

First broadcast on Radio 3 (Study)
weekly on Thursdays at 7.00 p.m.
from 27 March to 15 May, 1969

Charles Fox is jazz critic of the 'New Statesman' and has also written
for 'The Guardian' and 'The Sunday Times'. He reviews records for
'The Gramophone'. He has a weekly radio programme, 'Jazz Today',
in Music Programme and his broadcasts in Third Programme have
included series on 'The Three Faces of Jazz', 'The Music of Duke
Ellington', 'The Jazz Avant-Garde' and 'Poetry and Jazz'.

M L
3 5 6 1
. J 3 F 6 8

© Charles Fox 1969
First published 1969
Published by the British Broadcasting Corporation
35 Marylebone High Street, London W.1.
Printed in England
by Eyre and Spottiswoode Limited,
at The Thanet Press, Margate, Kent.
SBN: 563 08447 2

CONTENTS

INTRODUCTION

To many otherwise cultured people jazz is still something of an enigma. Part of the trouble springs from a fundamental misconception of what the music sets out to do. The single, most important fact to be grasped is that jazz is essentially an art of performance. A symphony or a sonata, leaving aside nuances of interpretation, possess the same kind of entity whoever happens to perform them. In jazz the situation is totally different. There it is the musicians, the performers, who give the music its identity. If the history of European concert music can be represented by a list of composers, then the history of jazz is a catalogue of performers. Which does not mean that jazz cannot be composed. The work of Jelly Roll Morton, Duke Ellington, Charles Mingus and a body of other composers proves it to be possible. Nevertheless, a jazz composition in the truest sense cannot be disentangled from the musicians performing it.

A present-day recording of *Black and Tan Fantasy* by the Duke Ellington Orchestra will communicate a different atmosphere from that band's original 1927 version, simply because the personnel has changed, the soloists are not the same. The overall structure remains, but the timbres and emotional undertones will have altered. To hear the piece played by, say, the Count Basie Orchestra would be to experience something very alien from Ellington's conception, for the whole character of Basie's band is different. Finally, a performance by an ensemble made up of players from a symphony orchestra would, quite simply, not be jazz at all. However skilled these musicians, they could not provide those subtleties that jazz performers contribute without thinking. Jazz, in fact, even composed jazz, is always the work of particular people.

It is frequently pointed out that African Music has played a big part in shaping jazz, and indeed its influence permeates a good deal of early jazz, yet even there the melodies and harmonies – with the exception of a deviation found in blues – are essentially European, based upon the diatonic scale. Rhythmically, too, almost all early jazz is metrically regular, usually in common time, although musicians occasionally ventured into $\frac{3}{4}$ and $\frac{6}{8}$. (It has only been during the past couple of decades that jazz has adopted more complex time-signatures.)

That elusive but far from mythical quality called 'swing' was not present in the earliest New Orleans period, when the music was closest to ragtime and used syncopation – with its emphasis on the two 'off' beats – extensively and with varying degrees of obviousness. 'Swing' became a detectable if wayward element in a jazz performance later on – certainly by the early 1920s – when it was possible for all four beats in the bar to be given equality. André Hodeir, the French critic, has described it as the balance of tension and relaxation. It certainly seems to be related to the African's – and by derivation, the jazz musician's – awareness that the placing of a note in time is every bit as important as its pitch and timbre. The way, for example, a great jazz musician like Louis Armstrong aligns his notes in relation to the regular pulse imbues them with a light but powerful impetus, a marvellous buoyancy. And this is what is meant by 'swing' – although it must be felt to be understood.

Where jazz also differs radically from European concert music is in its reliance upon improvisation. Yet even here one must be careful. Improvisation, in the sense of elaborate, on-the-spot variations upon a tune or set of chords, is not essential. There must, however, always be an element of extemporisation, a degree of spontaneity which will change an emphasis here, a note-value there, and keep a performance fresh and unique.

A jazz soloist improvises in several ways. One species of performer – Bix Beiderbecke is a good example, and so, but less consistently, is Sonny Rollins – uses the melodic line as the basis of his improvisation, producing either a paraphrase or the kind of elaboration familiar to concert-goers as a 'variation upon a theme'. The other species – more common, perhaps, in modern jazz – will base a solo entirely upon the harmonic sequence, often constructing a melodic line that differs completely from the original tune yet which shares the same chords. Coleman Hawkins was an early devotee of this method; it also under-lies the work of Charlie Parker. Other soloists – Louis Armstrong for one – use a mixture of the two approaches, producing solos that often bear some relation to the theme but which also contain material derived solely from the harmonic structure.

Another element, foreign to the European concert tradition but vital to jazz, is the use of vocalised tone by players of brass and reed instruments. This can be found in the folk music of many countries, a result of the performer trying to re-create the flexible characteristics of the human voice. Its presence in jazz is partly due to the music's African origins, partly to the fact that jazz was created by performers who were often unfamiliar with European conventions. It was vocalised tone that gave Johnny Dodds's clarinet playing its exciting shrillness, which produced Sidney Bechet's wide vibrato on the soprano saxophone, that inspired the bizarre effects obtained with plunger mutes by the trumpet and trombone soloists in Duke Ellington's orchestra. The tradition is still very much alive. It is, indeed, experiencing something of a renaissance at the hands of such avant-garde players as Ornette Coleman, Archie Shepp and Albert Ayler. In fact, leaving aside the efforts of certain white performers – first at the end of the 1920s and later during the 1950s – who sought to tidy up the music, the jazz musician tends to be highly idiosyncratic in his choice of timbres, of timing, of phrasing. Where the symphony or chamber music performer aims at impersonality, the jazz player cherishes his eccentricities. And it is this sense of identity, this emphasis upon individual uniqueness, that gives jazz its special quality, and makes its greatest musicians – men like Louis Armstrong and Miles Davis, Coleman Hawkins and Charlie Parker – instantly recognisable.

Another radical difference between jazz and European music has been the way the former lacks architectural shape. Jazz mostly exists as a strip in time, its metaphor the river rather than the cathedral. The ideal vehicle has been the twelve-bar blues, capable of being repeated again and again, for as long or as little as the musicians want to go on. The other basic pattern has been the 16 or 32 bar framework of the popular song. Only recently have jazz players started using other structures – sometimes more complex, sometimes much more flimsy – as a basis for their improvising.

Yet as well as differences, there are also similarities between European music and jazz. The most striking is the way jazz seems to have duplicated, although on a smaller scale and at a much more hectic pace, the same pattern of development. First there were the beginnings in folk song. Next came a polyphonic period, represented by the improvising of the New Orleans front-line. The introduction of written orchestrations was followed by the expansion of romanticism –

by Duke Ellington, as a composer, and Coleman Hawkins, as a soloist. Since then jazz has moved through neo-classical and neo-romantic phases and has begun its attempts at escape from conventional harmonic disciplines.

Most of the points made so far have been musical distinctions. But the history of jazz is also a series of reactions to social change and economic pressures, in which events such as the boll-weevil biting into the cotton crop and the repeal of Prohibition have all had an effect. As well as considering the styles and influences of the most important musicians, those who have imprinted themselves upon the fabric of jazz, it is also necessary to remember that none of them operated in a vacuum. Just as much as the minor performers – the drummer in the street band, the Kansas City blues shouter, the sideman in the swing orchestra – they were creatures of their time. It is this blend of the personal and the social, the aesthetic and the economic, that makes jazz reflect our century so faithfully.

Meanwhile the functions of jazz and of the jazz performer have changed drastically. During the earliest period in New Orleans, jazz was essentially a social music, used for a wide variety of purposes. In the 1920s and 1930s its scope narrowed; it became entertainment music, an accomplice of show business, designed purely for dancing or to be listened to in theatres and bars. The jazz musician was hired as an entertainer, and if he got away with something more – as Duke Ellington or Earl Hines or Coleman Hawkins certainly did – that was a tribute to his integrity as well as his cunning. Not until the 1940s did the initiative pass from the audience to the performer. For the first time the jazz musician began thinking of his music as art and of himself as an artist. He was not necessarily better, either technically or aesthetically, than his predecessors, yet his attitude was radically different, and it led – logically, inescapably – to the present situation, where jazz also sports an avant-garde of dedicated young players whose work appeals chiefly to a minority public.

Jazz has grown up alongside cinema, radio, television and the gramophone. Indeed, without the gramophone and radio it seems unlikely that the music would have spread outside, or even across, the United States. At first jazz travelled slowly, up the Mississippi aboard the riverboats, westward along the railroad tracks, wherever the earliest jazz bands were disposed to take it. Records and radio sets made the music less subject to the whims of chance and geography. For example, gramophone records enabled musicians in Europe to study, to emulate and eventually to challenge the American pioneers. They also brought a sense of immediacy, so that nowadays young European musicians can be aware almost instantly of what their counterparts are up to in Greenwich Village or San Francisco. The time-lag has been so reduced, that it now seems likely, let alone possible, that European musicians will themselves become innovators, influencing as well as being influenced.

All history is to some degree false, a gross simplification of what really happened. Jazz history certainly has its share of exaggerations. The trouble is that to convey some idea of how the music developed it is necessary to divide performers and events into styles and periods and geographical groupings. But these are only the most visible signs of what was really a much more complex and continuous process. Because a history of this kind dwells upon the innovators, the men who started new trends, it does not mean that earlier players packed their bags and slunk away. The rise of the big bands did not result in the total disappearance of the New Orleans performers, nor did the emergence of bebop put every swing musician out of work. One of the special delights of jazz is the coexistence that is feasible when an art has a life-span of scarcely more than half a century. After all, it is still possible – in a single city, even on a single concert platform – to see an archaic New Orleans band like George Lewis's, one of the large orchestras of the 1930s, such as Duke Ellington's, a bebop hero like Dizzy Gillespie or Thelonious Monk, and young avant-gardists like Archie Shepp or Albert Ayler. It is rather as if a festival might present Gregorian chant, a Mozart symphony, a Wagner opera and a smattering of Stockhausen all on the same night – and with each work conducted by its composer.

THE
BEGINNINGS

Jazz would not exist without Africa, yet it is not African music. Those African elements which it embraces are to be discovered in almost all American Negro, or Afro-American, music. The 'blues scale', for example, with its optional flattening of the third and seventh notes – the fifth too, quite often, usually in the minor scale – may have come about when Negro slaves, many of them accustomed to pentatonic (five-note) scales, tried to cope with European melodies based on the diatonic (seven-note) scale. The use of antiphony, the call-and-response pattern heard when a Negro congregation sings spirituals or gospel songs, is another common feature of African music. And both happen to be elements that have endured within jazz from the earliest times until the present day. To discover how they came to be part of jazz it is also necessary to find out how the Negro arrived in the United States.

An English slave-trading expedition under Sir John Hawkins took away a cargo of Africans as early as 1562, but not until the cultivation of rice and tobacco began in America two centuries later did the traffic in Negro slaves become really sizeable. Eli Whitney's invention of the cotton gin in 1795 changed the economic structure of the South, creating the big cotton plantations with their huge slave populations. During the 18th and early 19th centuries millions of Africans were seized and shipped to the Americas. Those who survived the voyage worked as slaves, either in Brazil, the West Indies, or – by far the largest proportion – in the Southern States.

Contrary to popular belief, the Africans had a highly developed culture of their own, one that centred around sculpture, music and the dance, that was functional and ritualistic rather than aesthetic. In America the slaves were taught to sing Protestant hymns, and on those European forms and harmonies they imposed their own traditions. The first result was the Negro spiritual. Many of the slaves had become converted to Christianity; they attended camp meetings where most of the hymns they sang were nonconformist-evangelical and emotional in mood and imagery. But Negro spirituals reflected not only religious faith, they also echoed the protest – necessarily veiled in symbolism – of an oppressed people. The chief concern of African music had been to recite the history of the tribe. The slave in America

12

Top right: Africa, showing areas from which slaves were drawn
Bottom right: Dancers and drummers of the Chuka Tribe

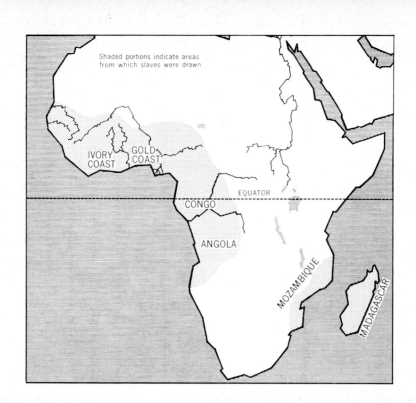

Shaded portions indicate areas
from which slaves were drawn

IVORY
COAST

GOLD
COAST

EQUATOR

CONGO

ANGOLA

MOZAMBIQUE

MADAGASCAR

discovered events in the Bible which paralleled his own situation. In *Go Down Moses* he was singing about a man who had led his people out of slavery; Canaan, the Israelites' Promised Land, became a vision of freedom. After the Northern armies had won the Civil War in 1865, and after the subsequent emancipation of the slaves, spirituals lost something of their urgency as protest songs. They survive, but in radically altered form. Yet this legal freedom brought with it fresh problems and new hardships, and some of these found expression in blues, the American Negro's most important secular and solo form of singing, an amalgam of spirituals and worksongs.

The worksong was exactly what its name suggests. For a man doing a hard physical job – chopping down trees, hammering in spikes, laying rails with a railroad gang – to sing in rhythm with the labour helped to make the work go easier. Today the worksong is extinct in all except a few remote areas of the United States – apart, that is, from inside the prison farms of the South. Blues are also largely self-descriptive. Ever since Elizabethan times, to have 'the blues' has implied a state of despondency. And Negro 'blues' have, more often than not, been sad, songs about loneliness or bad times, about the jinx that brings ill-luck, the lover who gets betrayed, the good times and the evil days. Boll-weevil, black snake or morning star – the images were close at hand, the themes nearly always personal, the singers at first anonymous: cotton-pickers, stevedores, railroad men. For them the blues became an emotional release, a way of facing up to life by singing about it. The form seems simple enough: a first line which gets repeated, followed by a third line that rhymes – more or less – with the other two:

> If you see me comin', hoist your window high,
> Oh, if you see me comin', hoist your window high,
> And if you see me goin', hang your head and cry.

The stanza is generally sung above a twelve-bar musical sequence, although there are alternative versions eight and sixteen bars long. And this relatively straightforward pattern not only formed the basis of the major American Negro song-form but has run like a spine throughout the entire history of jazz.

Gifted blues singers quickly found they could earn a living with their voices. Some began wandering through the Southern states,

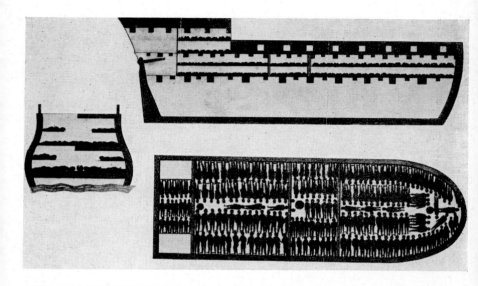

Top: Plan of a 19th century slave ship showing how slaves were packed in
Bottom: Bill advertising sale of negroes, c. 1850

a guitar slung over the shoulder. Of those singers whose names we know, one who was doing this during or just before World War I was Blind Lemon Jefferson from Texas, the first 'country blues' singer to get his music on record. But in the cities during the 1920s and 1930s the blues underwent a change. What had been casual became more rigid, what had been meditative and lyrical became more public, more dramatic both in form and content. And from being self-contained, providing his own guitar accompaniment, the professional blues artist now often used small groups of musicians. Men like Big Bill Broonzy, Sonny Boy Williamson and Leroy Carr, who worked in cities such as Chicago or Indianapolis, could not avoid producing a more sophisticated music than earlier generations of 'country' singers. But the 'classic blues' of the women singers illustrates the change at its most extreme. The first of these women singers, the one who bridges the gap, was 'Ma' Rainey – short, heavily-built, wearing a string of gold, twenty-dollar pieces round her neck – who sang in tent-shows all over the South.

17

Top left: Cotton picking in the southern states
Bottom left: Ma Rainey and her Georgia Band
Above: Record label c. 1928

Chords used in the earliest form of 12 bar blues.

In a typical Negro theatre of the 1920s the spotlight would pick out a brown-skinned woman dressed in satin, moving slowly across the stage, singing about the man who had deceived her, the rent that was overdue, the river that had flooded the town she lived in. It might be Bessie Smith or Ida Cox or Sara Martin – or one of the many lesser singers who flourished at the time, and whose relation with their public must have been as close as that which once prevailed in the English music-hall, when both singers and audience belonged to the same narrow community. The women blues singers frequently employed jazz musicians to accompany them (Ma Rainey and Bessie Smith both used Louis Armstrong on some records), but long before this the vocal and instrumental traditions of blues had converged and the harmonic sequence of the blues became a favourite basis for jazz players to improvise on. Understandably enough, blues – although not always the most genuine kind – attracted the attention of song publishers; W. C. Handy, a Negro bandleader from Memphis, collected and published a number of blues, including *St. Louis Blues*, but, ironically enough, the first song more or less in the blues idiom to appear in print was the work of a white man, Hart Wand, whose *Dallas Blues* was published in 1912.

Ragtime was another of the musical forms which contributed to jazz, despite the fact that it lies a little outside the main stream of American Negro music. It belongs, indeed, to the same area as the 19th century minstrel shows (usually the work of white entertainers), with their 'coon' songs and tap-dance routines. In fact, ragtime was a Negro response to a white demand. The period of pure ragtime lasted scarcely more than ten years, beginning with Tom Turpin's *Harlem Rag*, published in 1897, and Scott Joplin's *Original Rags*, which appeared two years later. The music – highly formal, heavily syncopated, essentially pianistic, allowing no scope at all for improvisation – flourished in and around St. Louis, the work of a small group of

18

Scott Joplin's 'Maple Leaf Rag'

talented pianist-composers. Later on ragtime was taken up by the
writers of popular songs, and also – much more significantly – by the
primitive jazz bands.

From ragtime jazz took syncopation, the accentuation of the weak
beats – usually 2 and 4 – in the bar, together with some of its melodic
material and its relatively elaborate structure, similar to the march
music of the period. From blues and spirituals jazz derived a certain
emotional strength and also a conception of modality, the so-called
'blues scale'. The third ingredient which helped in the creation of
jazz was the brass band, in particular the Negro marching bands of
the Southern states. Many bands of this sort had been organized just
after the Civil War, their musicians using those instruments discarded
by the bands of the Confederate and Union armies. (Something rather
similar happened in India after the withdrawal of the British Raj.)
These bands provided jazz with not only its early instrumentation but
also a tradition of brass playing, a tradition quickly reflected in the
high quality of early jazz performers on the cornet and trumpet.

These, then, were the separate strands which began drawing together
to make the music we know as jazz. But for the synthesis a time and
place were needed. The historical moment came about seventy years
ago. And it happened in a teeming, decidedly raffish seaport lying at
the mouth of the Mississippi River.

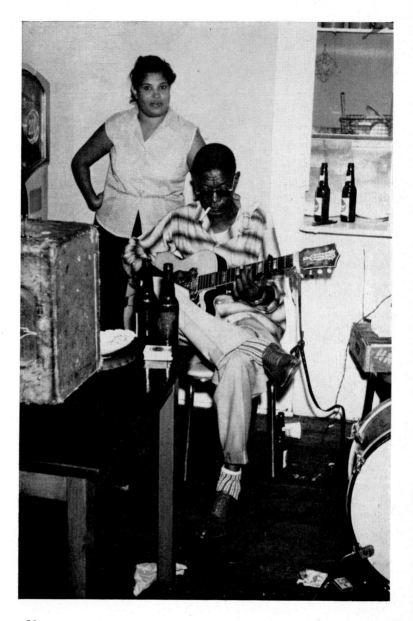

The Blues singer Lightnin' Hopkins
at the Sputnik bar, Houston, Texas in 1960

NEW ORLEANS

Legends, in the long run, are more persuasive than facts. And although Buddy Bolden, the cornet-playing barber of New Orleans, enjoyed a real, flesh-and-blood existence, his role in jazz history *is* almost legendary. For Bolden is the first outsized person one encounters, a man acknowledged to have been the original 'king' of New Orleans cornet players, his tone so powerful it could be heard twelve – or was it fourteen? – miles away. It has become difficult to separate apocrypha from truth, but certainly Bolden flourished from around 1895 until 1907, when he went berserk during a street parade. Eventually, many years later, he died in an asylum. Bolden was, in fact, the prototype of the tragic hero in jazz. the artist who burns himself out young, a part which has been enacted again and again. And in the case of Buddy Bolden there are no recordings to contradict the legend. His reputation is based on hearsay, on the memories of the musicians who knew him, musicians who were necessarily young at the time and in a hero-worshipping mood.

But hearsay is all we have to go on when reconstructing what happened during the early years of jazz. Claims have been made that jazz, or a music very like it, was being performed in other areas of the United States, particularly in other parts of the South, before the beginning of the century. That may be so. It is also true that jazz, although possibly not New Orleans jazz, began to be played in other towns soon after it became popular in New Orleans. The fact remains that even if jazz was not the exclusive creation of New Orleans, it was the musicians inhabiting that city who defined it, who gave it a formal and distinct identity.

First Spanish, then French, New Orleans finally came under the United States as part of the Louisiana Purchase of 1803. During the years that followed it developed into something of a boom town, the port used by all the prospectors moving in to open up the new territory. Throughout the 19th century New Orleans was really two cities: 'Uptown' was American, 'downtown' was French. And in addition to the blues and spirituals born from the blending of African with Protestant Anglo-Saxon music, New Orleans was privy to the mixing of African with Spanish and French idioms, a counterpart to the kind

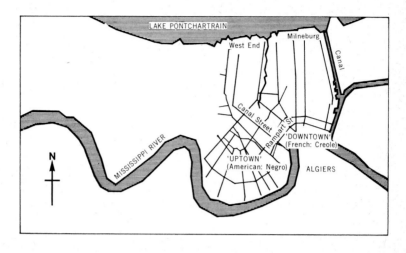

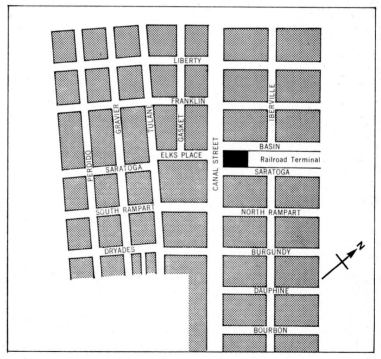

New Orleans with enlarged plan of Storyville area, c. 1910

of thing which happened in Cuba, Haiti and the West Indies. (Jelly Roll Morton has defined this element in jazz as 'the Spanish tinge'.) It is also worth remembering that *Tiger Rag* started life as an old French quadrille, much played in the Vieux Carré.

Just as cultures mingled, so did races. As well as the Negroes, descendants of the slaves, there were the coloured Creoles, a group that combined African with Spanish or French ancestry and which also inherited a European cultural background. It is not entirely coincidence that so many fine jazz clarinettists – men like Omer Simeon, Sidney Bechet and Albert Nicholas – should have been Creoles; not if you remember the tradition of reed-playing that pertained in France, and which existed in French New Orleans too. For example, Alphonse Picou, famous for his performances of the demanding clarinet solo in *High Society* – it was actually adapted from a piccolo part by another clarinettist, George Baquet – took lessons from the flautist at the French Opera House. The Negro slaves, on the other hand, had assembled every Saturday and Sunday afternoon in Congo Square (a field just off Rampart Street) almost regularly from just after the American occupation until the Civil War. According to a contemporary report, they danced and sang to the improvised music of 'drums, tom-toms and asses jaws'. After the Civil War came the rise of the Negro brass bands. By the end of the century there were certainly ragtime bands in existence in the city; one was led by a white man, 'Papa' Jack Laine. But whereas ragtime was always played as written, jazz used improvisation. And at some point jazz as we understand it came into being.

There is a measure of extemporisation in most folk musics of the world, but very often it is only a matter of embellishment, of the variation of a phrase, the accenting of a note. The earliest species of jazz improvising was of this sort; indeed, even today there are bands in New Orleans performing an archaic style of jazz which rarely ventures beyond this kind of ornamentation. The extent to which jazz improvising as we know it was present in the earliest New Orleans jazz remains a matter of conjecture; there are only the gramophone records from 1917 onward and the reminiscences of the musicians themselves. The indication is that performers of the calibre of Louis Armstrong and King Oliver and Johnny Dodds must have been using what was

23

Three part improvising on 'Panama' by the Kid Ory Creole Band

substantially the same approach – building independent solo lines –
for at least a number of years before they moved to Chicago and made
their earliest recordings.

At first the improvising was entirely collective: a practice which
encouraged the division of duties between cornet (or trumpet),
clarinet and trombone, the classic triumvirate of New Orleans jazz.
The cornet (or trumpet) played lead, sticking closest to the tune, while
the clarinet weaved patterns up above and the trombone filled in the
harmonies down below or interjected phrases designed to thrust the
group forward. The band would be completed by banjo (or guitar),
bass (either brass or string) and drums, with sometimes a piano as well.
The next decade was to bring an increase of individuality, but for the
time being the musicians subordinated themselves to the ensemble.
And the function of the music was not – as became the case later on –
confined to the dance-hall or theatre, but was social in the widest

Top left: 19th century bird's-eye view of New Orleans
Bottom left: Canal Street, New Orleans

Marching band in New Orleans

sense. 'There were countless places of enjoyment that employed musicians', recalls the guitarist Danny Barker, 'as well as private affairs, balls, soirees, banquets, marriages, deaths, christenings, Catholic communions, confirmations, picnics at the lake front, country hay rides, and advertisements of business concerns'.[1] Similarly, most of the musicians had day jobs. Zutty Singleton, himself a great drummer, has said: 'They were bricklayers and carpenters and cigar makers and plasterers. Some had little businesses of their own – coal and wood and vegetable stores. Some worked on the cotton exchange and some were porters'.[2] King Oliver even worked as a butler. The image, then, is slightly idyllic, of citizens performing a music accepted by their society – and performing it for all kinds of occasions. Like most idylls, however, it is not the complete truth. New Orleans society was as violent as it was unequal. And until the U.S. Navy Department closed it down in 1917, it was Storyville, the New Orleans licensed quarter (the first and last experiment of its kind in an American city), that provided work for the majority of local jazz musicians. The piano 'professors', men like Tony Jackson and the young Jelly Roll Morton, played in the 'sporting houses', while the bands generally worked at dance halls.

[1] *Hear me talkin' to ya* (1955).
[2] *Ibid*

The George Lewis Band outside Preservation Hall

Meanwhile the dynastic structure of New Orleans jazz was being perpetuated. When Buddy Bolden broke down in 1907, his successor as 'king' of the cornet players was Freddy Keppard, whose Olympia Band was among the finest in the city. One of Keppard's later bands would have been the first jazz group ever to get on record – in 1916 – if Keppard had not turned down the gramophone company's offer; he was afraid other people might steal his music. So the first New Orleans band to be recorded was a white group, the Original Dixieland Jazz Band. It was also the first jazz band to make an impression in New York, and the first to get to Europe (it opened at the London Hippodrome in the revue, 'Joy Bells', starring George Robey, on April 7, 1919). But the Original Dixielanders, just like the other white New Orleans groups, emphasized the ragtime element, pointing up the syncopation. With one or two exceptions, notably the clarinettists Leon Rapollo and Sidney Arodin, white New Orleans musicians could not play blues with either the intensity or elegance of the best Negro or Creole performers. On the other hand, not all the coloured New Orleans orchestras played jazz. The bands of A. J. Piron and Joseph Robichaux, both Creole groups, often included violins and performed music that appealed to the fashionable white audiences of the period.

27

Jazz did not develop at all tidily. It was a casual progression, a matter of musicians leaving the city, playing aboard riverboats and being heard in Natchez and Vicksburg and Memphis and St. Louis, or else taking their music up to Chicago or out to the West Coast. Freddy Keppard left New Orleans as early as 1911, although he returned from time to time. His place as the foremost bandleader was taken by Edward 'Kid' Ory, a musician usually credited with originating the slurring 'tailgate' style of trombone playing. Ory's band included most of the celebrated New Orleans musicians of those early years: his clarinettists were, successively, Big Eye Louis Nelson, Sidney Bechet, Johnny Dodds, Jimmy Noone, Wade Whaley and George Lewis, while the cornetist 'Papa' Mutt Carey was replaced by Joe Oliver, and then, when Oliver went to Chicago in 1917, by Louis Armstrong. Joe Oliver is the third great name in the dynasty of New Orleans cornet players but his biggest impact upon the music was to be made in the North. By the time he left New Orleans the musical scene was changing. America had entered World War I, Storyville had been closed down, unemployment was widespread in the South, yet plenty of jobs were to be found in the cities of the North. It was not surprising that jazz followed the drift of the Negro population, away from the elegant sea-port of its birth to the congested tenements and bedraggled streets of Chicago, the Windy City, the ugly goliath of the Midwest.

Original Dixieland Jazz Band, Hammersmith Palais, 1919

Tony Jackson

CHICAGO
AND KANSAS CITY

Even before World War I agriculture in the South had been in a bad way, with the far from legendary boll-weevil destroying the cotton crops. On the other hand, industry was expanding in the Middle West and along the Atlantic seaboard, and the outbreak of war in Europe only speeded this up. Between 1910 and 1920 nearly a million people (white as well as black) migrated to the North. The population of the Black Belt, the Negro area lying on the South side of Chicago, doubled within five years. This meant that by the beginning of the 1920s there was a large audience for musicians and entertainers in the Northern cities, and particularly in Chicago. And just as the closing-down of Storyville in 1917 had meant fewer jobs for jazz musicians in New Orleans, so, by an ironic counter-stroke, the enactment of Prohibition in 1920 ushered in whole chains of 'speak-easies' and illicit drinking clubs. It is unfortunate but undeniable that jazz has often flourished most vigorously in corrupt surroundings. It was true in Chicago during the 1920s, and in Kansas City for an even longer period. The free-and-easy attitude of the civic authorities allowed club-owners to do more or less as they liked, which in turn meant plenty of jobs for musicians. At the same time the function of jazz narrowed considerably. The same musicians who in New Orleans had played for all kinds of community activities now rarely worked outside the night club, the theatre or the dance-hall.

Two men dominated the early part of the decade: King Oliver and Louis Armstrong. Both came from New Orleans, both played the cornet, both exerted an enormous influence upon their contemporaries. Otherwise there were vast differences between them, temperamentally and in the fates which lay ahead of them. Armstrong went on to become the rich and admired entertainer who is still hard at work today; Oliver died in 1938, sick and penniless, an odd-job man at a billiard hall in Savannah. But in 1922 Oliver was at the peak of his fame, and Armstrong, just fifteen years younger, was giving signs of the brilliance to come. The two men played side by side in Oliver's Creole Jazz Band, a band with a particular genius – if genius can be shared collectively – for ensemble improvisation. Oliver's band brought the classic New Orleans pattern to the highest, most turbulent point

30

Top right: Bix Beiderbecke (2nd from extreme right) and
The Wolverines in Gennett Studios, Richmond, Indiana, 1924
Bottom right: Louis Armstrong and his All Stars in London, 1956

it ever reached. There were a few solos – good ones, too – but the group's real vitality came from the dialogue that went on inside the front-line. Hearing that band in the flesh was a catalytic experience for many young white musicians.

'Take a composite of, first the New Orleans Rhythm Kings, who planted the seed', says the tenor saxophonist Bud Freeman, recalling those days, 'And then Joe Oliver, Louis Armstrong, Bix, Jimmy Noone and Bessie Smith. Our style, 'Chicago style', came from all of that.'[1] It was the work of white men – Frank Teschemacher, Muggsy Spanier, Eddie Condon, Mezz Mezzrow and others – who tried in their own way to recreate the intensity of New Orleans jazz. For a start, they altered the balance of the front-line, keeping the trumpet and clarinet – indeed, the clarinet became the dominant instrument – but often using a saxophone instead of a trombone. In some ways 'Chicago style' was not so much a style as a collision of sympathetic musicians, almost a forerunner of the jam session. The music came out sounding tough and brittle and slightly bitter, a perfect reflection of the society in which it was created, the mobsters' jungle bossed by Al Capone and Dion O'Banion. Most of these musicians had to earn their living in commercial dance bands, and were more frustrated artistically than their black counterparts; their situation was that of a dedicated avant-garde, heard only on occasional records and at casual sessions. Bix Beiderbecke moved among, and was an influence upon, this little circle, although he never recorded with them. Beiderbecke came from Davenport and had learnt his jazz by listening to riverboat bands and records of the Original Dixieland Jazz Band. His playing was lyrical, his style an early example of romanticism at work in jazz, yet almost alone among the important soloists, perhaps because his roots lay in white Dixieland music, Beiderbecke never distinguished himself as a blues player. It was, too, his fate to spend a large chunk of his career performing in successful but inhibiting dance orchestras; first with Jean Goldkette, then with Paul Whiteman, the most popular bandleader of the 1920s.

Yet the musical achievements in Chicago that pointed towards the future were the work of two New Orleans men, Jelly Roll Morton and Louis Armstrong. In New Orleans, Morton had excelled as a solo pianist; in Chicago his great contributions were made as a bandleader

[1]*Hear me talkin' to ya* (1955).

32

and composer. Behind the bragadoccio and the flashing diamond tooth, Morton was a sensitive musician, the first genuine jazz composer, his major works the records he made with his Red Hot Peppers between 1926 and 1928. Whenever possible he used New Orleans musicians and retained the classic New Orleans instrumental balance, yet he converted both the players and the convention into vehicles for his own ideas. What Morton really did was to dramatize the New Orleans ensemble, moulding the improvisation to his personal ends (he would indicate to a soloist the general effect he wanted), plotting in advance the shape and sound of a performance.

Louis Armstrong's introduction to 'West End Blues'

If Morton's records represent the harnessing of soloists and ensemble style to the imagination of a single man, those by Louis Armstrong's Hot Five and Seven reveal a great soloist elbowing his way out of the New Orleans ensemble. The earliest – made in 1925 and 1926 – come closest to traditional New Orleans practices. Then, bit by bit, Armstrong emerges as a virtuoso, at first through his dazzling breaks and stop-time choruses, finally becoming the focus and climax of the performance rather than one strand in its development. By 1928 he was recording with his Savoy Ballroom Five, a group that included the pianist Earl Hines, another musician of great quiddity, using neat little arrangements written by Don Redman. The 1930s were to see Armstrong move further and further away from his musical beginnings, often exaggerating the more sensational aspects of his technique, revealing – like many jazz musicians of his generation – a flair for showmanship, developing into a singer of rare amiability and charm. But it is not just because he was the first great individual

33

soloist that Armstrong looms enormous in jazz history; using what was a fairly simple harmonic basis, he built up solos of remarkable imaginative breadth and emotional tenseness. His style was explicit, classical in its ordering of parts, its apparent inevitability, and to that extent a splendid example for others to follow. Armstrong created, in fact, a vocabulary of jazz improvisation, a method of playing solos that was taken over by most of his contemporaries – trombonists, pianists and saxophonists as well as trumpeters.

But if the Negroes living on Chicago's South Side went to hear Louis Armstrong at the Vendome Theatre, if they danced to King Oliver at the Lincoln Gardens, or bought the latest Jelly Roll Morton disc, they also had the blues more or less on their doorsteps. And not just the singers. Chicago saw the maturing of boogie-woogie, a style of piano playing that was despised as low-life music by a good many jazz musicians (Jelly Roll Morton is reported to have been offended when asked to play it). In its way, boogie-woogie was severely functional, designed to cut through the chatter and noise of the backrooms and dives where it was usually performed. Its chief identifying characteristic was the ostinato bass, frequently but not necessarily employing eight notes to the bar, against which the pianist's right hand improvised sharp, percussive phrases. Jimmy Yancey, who worked for many years as ground-keeper at the Chicago White Sox baseball park, played an early, much more lilting version of the style, his bass figures often reminiscent of the *habanera*, the whole performance close to the spirit of country blues. The pianists who came after him, men like Pinetop Smith, Meade Lux Lewis, Cripple Clarence Lofton and Albert Ammons, defined the style, giving it a hardness and forcefulness that fitted its surroundings.

Meade Lux Lewis's 'Honky Tonk Train Blues'

Boogie-woogie was, of course, an adaptation for piano of blues guitar playing, a latterday example of the same process which saw lute music transcribed for the harpsichord in the 17th century. Its

34

Top right: King Oliver's Creole Jazz Band, 1922
(Louis Armstrong is 4th from the left)
Bottom right: Albert Ammons

origins lay in the mining-towns and railroad construction camps of the Southwest, as well as larger, prosperous centres like St. Louis and Kansas City. Just after World War I it was still being called 'Fast Western' because it flourished in the state of Texas and in towns on the western side of the Mississippi river. But this territory always had a strong blues tradition. It produced Blind Lemon Jefferson, and afterwards such performers as Big Bill Broonzy, Texas Alexander and – much later on – Joe Turner. Jazz bands working the area were also expected to feature a high proportion of blues in their programmes, with audiences showing disapproval if they failed to do so.

This huge geographical complex, hinging on Kansas City and taking in the states of Texas, Arkansas, Missouri, Kansas and Oklahoma, witnessed some lively developments during the 1920s and 1930s. The early bands seem to have played New Orleans music, but by the mid-1920s there were nine- and ten-piece orchestras, using sections of brass and reeds, just as there were in Chicago and New York. And quite early on their music displayed characteristics that became associated with Southwestern bands. There was the 'riff', a one- or two-bar phrase, repeated again and again, either behind a soloist or to build up an obsessive excitement. 'Riffs' were found in ragtime, and before that in African music, but it was bands like Walter Page's Blue Devils and Bennie Moten's Kansas City Orchestra that really conscripted them into jazz. (Later on, in New York in the 1930s, the riff became an integral part of the swing era, helped by the arrival on the East Coast of Count Basie's band – yet another Kansas City group.) Another favourite device was the chase chorus, in which two soloists alternated, taking four or two bars apiece.

Riff Pattern: Bennie Moten's 'Toby'

There were plenty of good bands in the Southwest. Jesse Stone kept touring Missouri and Kansas, Troy Floyd worked down in San Antonio, and Alphonse Trent was based in Dallas. (Some idea of these bands' popularity can be judged from the fact that Trent's sidemen

37

Top: Map showing principal centres of early Jazz activities
Bottom: Bennie Moten's Kansas City Orchestra, Fairyland Park,
Kansas City, 1931

were earning $150 a week and driving round in Cadillacs.) Many of them travelled vast distances to play one-night stands, and they battled with one another – musically, that is – in the dance-halls, just as New Orleans bands once strove to out-blow each other in the streets. (After Jesse Price's group lost a bout with Walter Page's Blue Devils it was more or less forced to disband.) But just as New Orleans had summarized the kind of music being played around the South at the start of the century, so the jazz of the Southwest took definitive form in the work of Kansas City bands like those of Bennie Moten and Andy Kirk. Moten's orchestra, in particular, dominated this musical scene. In the 1920s it leaned towards ragtime, and was notable for loose section work and fairly uncomplicated solos, but by the early 1930s Moten was deploying riffs in an unusually fierce and imaginative fashion, and using soloists like Ben Webster, Hot Lips Page and Bill (not yet 'Count') Basie.

'Some places in Kansas City never closed,' recalls Jo Jones, Count Basie's drummer. 'You could be sleeping one morning at 6 a.m. and a travelling band would come into town for a few hours. Then they would wake you up to make a session with them until eight in the morning.'[1] It was a stimulating atmosphere. Indeed, for jazz musicians of the 1920s and 1930s Kansas City must have seemed a sort of premature Elysium, yet the basis of its tolerance rested, just like that of Chicago, in corruption. The regime of Thomas J. Pendergast, the most powerful American political boss of his generation, extended from 1927 until 1938. During that period Kansas City was a wide-open town, with the authorities positively encouraging gambling and night-life. Clubs like the Sunset, where Joe Turner shouted blues as well as served the drinks, were the setting for those jam sessions. If the Fletcher Henderson band was passing through, then Coleman Hawkins or Chu Berry would be busy defending their reputations, while the local tenor players – Ben Webster and Dick Wilson and Lester Young – tried to cut them down to size.

This mixture of competition and camaraderie went on well into the 1930s, undeterred by either the violence – it was in Kansas City that Pretty Boy Floyd machine-gunned four policemen – or the civic squalor. Nevertheless, by 1939, when Thomas Pendergast was committed to prison for income tax evasion, things had begun to

[1]*Ibid.*

change. Yet the influence of the Southwest upon jazz history was far from ended. Count Basie's band was in New York. A brilliant young guitarist, Charlie Christian, had left Oklahoma City to work with Benny Goodman. Jimmy Blanton from St. Louis was just about to join Duke Ellington's orchestra and to revolutionize the whole craft of jazz bass playing. Meanwhile, back in Kansas City, in the ranks of Jay McShann's band, a group thoroughly steeped in the Southwest blues tradition, there was an alto saxophonist called Charlie Parker. But that is to jump ahead a little too far.

The old Sunset Cafe (now renamed the Grand Terrace) on the southwest corner of 35th Street and Calumet Avenue, Chicago. Louis Armstrong and other great jazz men played here in the 1920s

NEW YORK

New Orleans jazz grew out of a complex social environment. In Chicago and Kansas City jazz was a response to the demands of a wide, popular audience. But in New York the jazz musician found himself in more direct contact with naked commercial incentives. For New York was the centre of the record industry and the theatre circuits; it also housed the offices of the music publishers and variety agents. New York, in fact, was the place to which all ambitious young song-writers headed as soon as they could raise the fare. It was on Broadway, after all, that 'Running Wild' was staged, an all-Negro show with music by James P. Johnson, not merely a great jazz pianist but the man who started Americans and Europeans dancing the Charleston. And to New York hurried those musicians—well, principally the white ones – who wanted steady, well-paid work as session-men or playing in pit orchestras. The late Iain Lang once pointed out that the vital difference between Negro singers, dancers and musicians in New York and their humbler counterparts in New Orleans before World War I was that Buddy Bolden and Freddy Keppard played to Negro audiences, while Bert Williams was a Ziegfield star and Will Marion Cook took violin lessons from Joachim. Similarly, the Fletcher Henderson orchestra achieved its early success playing for white dancers at the Roseland Ballroom on Broadway, and it was to white audiences that the Duke Ellington band performed during the years it spent at the Cotton Club.

There had been large, so-called 'jazz orchestras' in New York before Fletcher Henderson became a bandleader. James Weldon Johnson has written of a concert given by the Memphis Students in 1905: 'It was a playing-singing-dancing orchestra, making dominant use of banjos, mandolins, guitars, saxophones and drums. . . . There was also a violin, a couple of brass instruments and a double bass. . . . They introduced the dancing conductor.'[1] Minstrel or ragtime orchestras of this sort must have been common in New York before and during World War I. But Henderson organised the first large band to provide an orchestral counterpart to the improvising jazz ensemble, replacing the counterpoint of the New Orleans front-line with harmonised section work, yet leaving space for solos. In New

[1]JAMES WELDON JOHNSON: *Black Manhattan* (1930)

40

Orleans the trombone had played a strictly functional role; now, in the hands of Henderson's trombonist, Jimmy Harrison – and those of white musicians like Miff Mole and Jack Teagarden – the instrument began to sound almost as agile and flexible as a trumpet. But the Henderson sideman who exerted most influence upon the future was Coleman Hawkins. A tradition already existed for brass instruments, but saxophones were late arrivals. Hawkins himself has always denied that he was the first man to play jazz on the tenor saxophone, and no doubt this is true, yet he was the first soloist of any quality, and he created a style and method for others to copy. By 1929 he was using the extravagant, semi-rhapsodic manner that is linked with his name, making great use of arpeggiation yet not being trapped by it. By the time he left for Europe in 1934 Hawkins had achieved an exquisite balance in his solos, a perfect blending of the lyrical and the dramatic.

James P. Johnson

It was over roughly the same period that Duke Ellington developed his methods of composition. 'You can't write music right,' he once told a fellow-passenger during the rail journey from Cleveland to Pittsburgh, 'unless you know how the man that'll play it plays poker.' By this Ellington meant that he composed with individual musicians in mind, putting together unique timbres, personal sounds, rather than just scoring the notes of a chord or thinking simply in terms of trumpets, trombones, clarinets and saxophones. When Ellington arrived in New York from Washington his ambition was to become a songwriter. It is arguable that had he not taken a band into the Cotton Club he might never have become the composer that he is. For Ellington was faced with the task of having to provide background music for the floor-shows. And the Twenties were curious years. A youth-cult was in full swing, just as one is today, and the primitive – or what was imagined to be primitive – was highly fashionable. According to the Negro poet Langston Hughes, thousands of white socialites trekked up to Harlem night after night, thinking the Negroes loved to have them there, believing that all Harlemites left their houses at sundown to sing and dance in cabarets. In fact, the Cotton Club did not allow Negroes in at all – as patrons, that is. And Ellington provided the music for a revue which pivoted around the notion that Harlem was only a step away from darkest Africa. What was more fitting than the trumpet snarls, the trombone growls, the whole armoury of bizarre effects which Ellington bent to his own aesthetic ends? For a time the orchestra even recorded as 'The Jungle Band'. It was, ironically, these very pressures which provided Ellington with the elements of his composing style, just as later commercial pressures continued to give his music shape and direction. Left to himself, Ellington might very easily have floundered in romanticism and produced only second-rate rhapsodies.

When the Spanish poet, Federico Garcia Lorca, visited Harlem in 1929 he described it as 'A great king held captive, dressed like a janitor'. Nancy Cunard took a different view. On seeing Seventh Avenue she wrote, 'I thought of the Mile End Road – the same long vista, the same kind of little, low houses, the same amount of blowing dust, papers, litter . . .'[1] Harlem is not the only Negro community in New York. There is another at Brooklyn, still another – Jamaica – at

[1]*Negro* (edited by Nancy Cunard) (1934).

Top right: Duke Ellington Band, 1931
Bottom right: Entrance to The Cotton Club, New York

Queen's. But Harlem is the biggest urban Negro community in the world. Negroes began moving in around 1900, when it was still a white area. The houses needed rebuilding, the transport services were bad, but by 1920 200,000 Negroes were living in Harlem; by the early 1930s there were 350,000. And despite the six or seven millionaires who resided on Sugar Hill or on 139th Street ('Strivers' Row'), most Harlemites worked hard, lived humbly and never saw the inside of a night club unless they worked there. To pay the rent they often held parlour-socials, parties that guests paid to attend. 'A hundred people would crowd into one seven-room flat until the walls bulged', says Willie 'The Lion' Smith, 'Food! hog maws (pickled pig bladders) and chitt'lin's with vinegar – you never ate nothing until you ate them. . . . When we played the shouts, everyone danced.'[1] James P. Johnson, Willie 'The Lion', Fats Waller (the boy organist from the 134th Street Subway Baptist Church), Duke Ellington – all performed at Harlem parlour socials just after World War I. And it was James P. Johnson who transformed the fragile patterns of ragtime, filling out the chords, borrowing a little from the blues, creating a percussive, striding, essentially self-contained style of playing that is still called 'Harlem Piano'.

It was these Harlemites who bet on the numbers game; who bought love-potions from High John the Conqueror and dream-books from Rajah Robo, a fire-eater; who queued outside the Lafayette Theatre to see Ethel Waters or Louis Armstrong or Butterbeans and Susie. And if they felt like dancing there was the Savoy Ballroom, Harlem's 'Home of Happy Feet'. 'Music rots when it gets *too* far from dancing', wrote Ezra Pound in his 'ABC of Reading'. It was a statement that scarcely needed uttering in Harlem. Bands like Chick Webb's and Luis Russell's, even those of Benny Carter and Don Redman, which went in for elaborate orchestrations, all played for a dancing public.

But New York jazz was not exclusively black music. The Original Dixieland Jazz Band had visited the city in 1917 and left behind a host of imitators. It became fashionable for these groups to be named after Southern states and cities, so bands calling themselves the Arkansas Travellers, the Savannah Six or the Tennessee Ten, catered for dancers or made records within the boundaries of New York State.

[1] RUDI BLESH & HARRIET JANIS: *They all played ragtime* (1958).

44

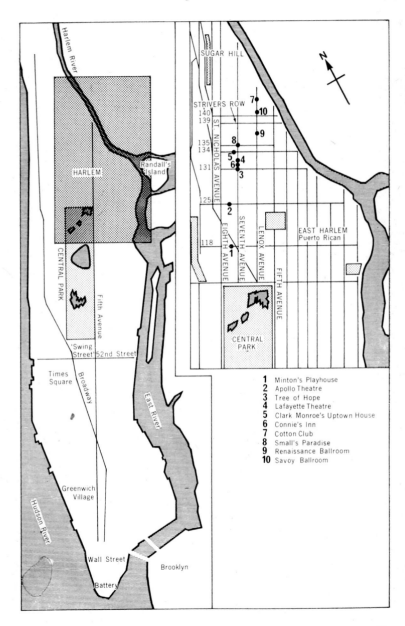

Map of Manhattan with inset showing street plan of Harlem

The musicianship of the best white players, session-men like Red Nichols, Miff Mole, Eddie Lang, Joe Venuti and the occasional 'outsider' like Jack Teagarden from Texas, was highly polished, their ideas were often elegant, and they could be heard on numerous discs by The Charleston Chasers, Red Nichols and his Five Pennies and Miff Mole and his Little Molers, all of them records that circulated widely in Britain as well as America and that formed the taste of the first generation of European jazz collectors. These are the denizens of Scott Fitzgerald's Jazz Age; the band that played at Gatsby's parties could easily have been the Original Memphis Five or the Birmingham Blue Buglers. But the time for frivolity was almost over. The Wall Street crash of 1929 rocked more than the stock market, and life for the majority of American citizens suddenly became much harsher. The best Negro players remained where most of them were already – up in Harlem. Those few white musicians who had played jazz for a living mostly retreated into the big commercial dance-bands. For the next few years jazz went underground.

Brass section of Lucky Millinder's Blue Rhythm Band, 1934. Henry 'Red' Allen (centre), J. C. Higginbotham (extreme left)

SWING

Prohibition was repealed throughout the United States in 1933. It meant the end of the speak-easies and the emergence of lots of small clubs with dance-floors and public bars which employed musicians. Similarly, the easing of the Depression halfway through the 1930s brought a psychological change, a revulsion against sentiment and self-pity which expressed itself in a dancing frenzy, a paroxysm as violent but light-hearted as the Charleston craze of a dozen years earlier It was this dancing-fever that Benny Goodman, a quiet-mannered, bespectacled clarinettist from Chicago, was to profit by, and which saw big band jazz make its way for the very first time into the 1930s equivalent of the Top Twenty.

Goodman organised his first regular band in 1935. It contained soloists like the trumpeter Bunny Berigan and the pianist Jess Stacy, and Goodman commissioned Fletcher Henderson – the man who had started the first big Negro jazz orchestra – to write a library of arrangements. These arrangements followed the same pattern as those Henderson had devised or procured for his own band, relying on a 'call-and-response' dialogue between brass and reeds. This antiphonal device, with roots in Negro gospel music and – long before that – in the mainstream of African music, was applied not only to tunes like Jelly Roll Morton's *King Porter Stomp*, one of Goodman's earliest 'hits', but to pop-songs of the present and past, pieces like *Blue Skies* and *Sometimes I'm Happy*.

There had been earlier attempts at projecting jazz to a wider audience – wider, that is, than the Negro dancers and the handful of white *aficionados*. The Dorsey Brothers Orchestra and Glen Gray's Casa Loma band both smuggled a fair amount of jazz material into programmes otherwise made up of sweeter, more conventional offerings. But the Benny Goodman band represented the first all-out effort at selling jazz to the public without making too many concessions. It was partly idealistic, with Goodman egged on by John Hammond, jazz critic, impresario and dedicated benefactor, and like many idealistic gestures it ended up by being hugely successful.

Any market researcher knows that for a product to sell it needs a label, and in this case it bore the name 'swing'. The word had cropped

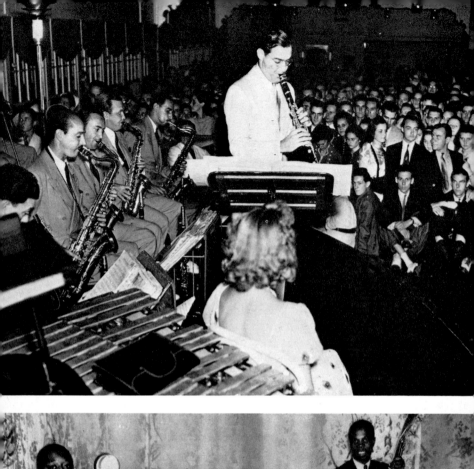

up before. In 1932 Duke Ellington's orchestra recorded *It Don't Mean A Thing If It Ain't Got That Swing*, its lyric referring to the quality that often distinguished a good from a bad jazz performance. Ellington, in fact, was using 'swing' in the same sense that Fats Waller did in the celebrated exchange of a few years later. ('Mr. Waller, what is swing?' asked the American matron, to which came the riposte: 'Lady, if you got to ask, you ain't got it.') By 1936, however, 'swing' was being used to describe a kind of music rather than a quality. Billie Holiday even recorded a song with the refrain: 'Once they called it ragtime, now they call it swing.' The image-makers had been busy.

Some notion of Benny Goodman's commercial success can be judged from the statistics of that day in March, 1937 when his band first performed at the Paramount Theatre in New York. By 3 p.m. 11,500 people had paid to go in, while the grand total for the day worked out at 21,000. Jitterbugging took place in the aisles. Goodman's was the first band to produce this sort of reaction but it was quickly followed by others, most of them playing safe and using a very similar formula. The earliest were the best, bands like those led by Artie Shaw, Tommy Dorsey, Charlie Barnet and Red Norvo. It is sadly significant that the most successful swing bands were all white; although Negro orchestras like Duke Ellington's and Jimmie Lunceford's were at their peak during this period, they never enjoyed anything like the same popularity. Nor did Count Basie's orchestra, which had arrived from Kansas City in the winter of 1936. The texture of Basie's music was, in any case, aggressive and rough-sounding compared with that of the other New York bands. Most of the time the band played 'head' arrangements, worked up by the musicians themselves, making great use of riffs, and loose enough to allow full-sized brass and reed sections to swing with a spontaneity which up to that time had been the monopoly of small groups. As with all good Kansas City bands, the rhythm section was a source of strength, the perfectly balanced quartet of Basie, Freddie Green, Walter Page and Jo Jones marking the four even beats like one man. The outstanding soloist, Lester Young, played the tenor saxophone in a way that was the first important reaction to an orthodoxy represented by Coleman Hawkins and his followers. Where Hawkins was warm and emotional, Young sounded detached, almost dispassionate, his tone pale, his phrasing lean, often

49

Top left: Benny Goodman Orchestra circa 1938
Bottom left: 'Fats' Waller and his Rhythm, recording in 1938

lagging a trifle behind the beat, or else anticipating it ever so slightly, a soloist who seemed at this time never to be at a loss for a flash of inspiration.

The colour-line had long ago broken down in recording studios. Now it began to be challenged in public. There were failures, like Mezz Mezzrow's attempt at leading a mixed group of black and white musicians at the Harlem Uproar House, which ended with swastikas daubed on the floors and ceiling. But Benny Goodman regularly used two remarkable Negro musicians – the pianist Teddy Wilson and the vibraphonist Lionel Hampton – in his Trio and Quartet. Hampton was among the earliest musicians to exploit the amplified or electrically operated instruments which began appearing during the 1930s. Another was Charlie Christian, not the first electric guitarist but certainly the one who popularised the instrument and developed a style which took into account its quirks and its virtues. Christian, too, worked for Goodman in the early 1940s, and he was, like Lester Young, very much a transitional figure, his roots in the music of the swing era but his solos pointing towards the jazz that was to supplant it. He was also a skilful concoctor of those riff-themes that were the bare bones of many performances by the Goodman Sextet.

Riff Pattern: Benny Goodman's 'A Smo-o-o-oth One'

Genuine jazz singers, as distinct from blues singers, have always been rarities. One who made a reputation during the 1930s was Mildred Bailey, the wife of Red Norvo and the first white girl to sing jazz at all convincingly. Another was Ella Fitzgerald, an orphan who had been discovered by Chick Webb at a talent contest at the Apollo Theatre. But by far the greatest was Billie Holiday. Like the other two, she reached maturity at a moment when blues and the earlier forms of jazz were in retreat, and what she did was to transfer the emotional climate of blues to the contemporary pop-song. By the slant of her voice, the placing of a syllable, she would translate what were often bathetic words into something close to poetry. And she

51

Top left: Jimmie Lunceford and his Orchestra
Bottom left: Count Basie and his Orchestra

Chord sequence of 12 bar blues played in the late 1930s

treated the musical framework as radically as any jazz soloist, breaking it down to basic elements, then reconstructing, moulding the line to suit her interpretation of the lyric. This use of pop-song material – the work of men like George Gershwin, Harold Arlen and Richard Rodgers, as well as the hacks of the period – was not confined to the singers of the 1930s but could be found in instrumental jazz as well.

Jazz bands had always made some use of contemporary pop-songs, even in New Orleans, but the Negro bands of the 1920s usually relied upon blues, rags, stomps and other compositions intended to be performed as jazz. Significantly enough, it was mostly the young white musicians in Chicago and New York who applied their jazz styles to tunes like *Nobody's Sweetheart, Ida* and *Some Of These Days*, material their audiences would be familiar with. And as jazz enlarged its area of activity this practice increased. In any case, it suited the talents of some performers. As early as 1929 Coleman Hawkin recorded a classic improvisation upon a pop-song, *If I Could Be With You One Hour Tonight*; ten years later, his recording of *Body And Soul* provided another superb example of the way in which a new identity could be grafted on to a familiar theme. A different, even more commercially viable approach was that mixture of bonhomie and joshing-up which musician-entertainers like Louis Armstrong and Fats Waller brought to the songs they performed. It was sound showmanship. It was also a way of getting across to an audience that might have been bored by the blues.

This was the kind of jazz – not too demanding, emphasizing technique, generally using tunes the white club-goers could identify – which got played on 52nd Street, the centre of jazz activity in New York from the early 1930s up to the mid-1940s, when property developers moved in and put up office-blocks. Lying just off Fifth

53

Top left: Lionel Hampton
Bottom left: Coleman Hawkins Band, Spotlite Club, 52nd Street, 1944 (Thelonious Monk is the pianist)

Avenue, this residential district had been honeycombed with speak-easies during Prohibition. Now it housed clubs like the Onyx, where Stuff Smith mixed comedy routines with violin playing, and where, earlier on, Art Tatum, worshipped by all his fellow-pianists, used to turn well-known themes into ornate structures of his own. Further along the Street could be heard musicians such as Henry 'Red' Allen, J. C. Higginbotham and Ed Hall, while Sidney Bechet, his hair prematurely white, played his soprano saxophone in a trio at Nick's. A barn-like room, full of stuffed birds in glass cases, with moth-eaten moose heads on the walls, Nick's was also the centre for those Chicagoans who had moved to New York. The bands there were recruited by Eddie Condon and usually included the clarinettist Pee Wee Russell, a virtuoso of unorthodoxy.

Nevertheless, just as in New Orleans, things were not so idyllic as they seemed. The big swing bands made plenty of money, yet few of the musicians on 52nd Street earned much more than a living wage. When the Spirits of Rhythm worked at the Onyx Club they were said to split $150 five ways. A top intermission pianist like Teddy Wilson might command $125 a week in the mid-1930s, while Billie Holiday, when she came to The Famous Door, young and not very well known, got around $100. And there were aesthetic grounds for dissatisfaction. Many of the big bands fell back on novelties, 'swinging the classics' (Tommy Dorsey's *Song of India* started the trend) or making orchestral adaptations of boogie-woogie. Young Negro musicians, fed up with the wellworn riffs, the same, simple chord changes, wanted to push the music into the future. Many white devotees, inspired by hearing Muggsy Spanier's Ragtimers or reading nostalgic history in the newly-published book, 'Jazzmen', wished to recreate the past. Whichever way they faced, the young were impatient and avid for change.

BEBOPPERS
AND REVIVALISTS

'No one man or group of men started modern jazz', Dizzy Gillespie has said. 'Some of us began to jam at Minton's in the early Forties. But there were always some cats showing up there who couldn't blow at all, but would take six or seven choruses to prove it. So on afternoons before a session, Thelonious Monk and I began to work out some complex variations on chords and the like. And we used them at night to scare away the no-talent guys.'[1] There was, of course, much more to it than that. No doubt the young musicians did want to get rid of the untalented. And as Negroes they resented the way that white musicians had – as some quite bluntly put it – 'stolen their music'. (What, they might argue, had swing been but white band-leaders cashing in on Negro jazz?). Yet in addition to this urge to make things difficult for the 'ofays' – pig-Latin for foe, meaning white men – and the mediocre, there was dissatisfaction with the static condition of jazz at the end of the swing era. And this was really the chief stimulus. Good artists, after all, expand technique not just for its own sake but in order to excite the imagination. Tension is created by the way content rubs against form.   [1] *Hear me talkin' to ya* (1955)

55

Thelonious Monk

Nevertheless, jazz did not change completely overnight. The process was gradual, without any conscious attempt at dramatic innovation. And it was not so much a revolution, the toppling of an existing structure, as a coup d'etat, a take-over. The setting for these experiments was New York City, the first laboratory Clark Monroe's Uptown House, where Charlie Parker sat in as early as 1939 and where Charlie Christian, Dizzy Gillespie, Budd Johnson, Jimmy Blanton and Kenny Clarke were often to be found. In the autumn of 1940 this little coterie moved its headquarters sixteen blocks downtown, to the Playhouse owned by Henry Minton, an ex-saxophonist. ('A rather drab place, frequented by old men', is how Kenny Clark remembers Minton's in its early days.) One of the first things to go was the balance inside the rhythm section. Where earlier drummers had stressed all four beats in the bar, Kenny Clarke – unquestionably the pioneer – used only his top cymbal for this, keeping the bass drum for accenting, for sudden explosions ('dropping bombs' was the contemporary – and topical – expression). Adopting a role already foreshadowed by Jimmy Blanton with Duke Ellington's band, the bassist now replaced the drummer as fulcrum of the rhythm section and marked those four beats to the bar. The pianist acted principally as a kind of harmonic guide, while the guitarist was eliminated from this new and severely functional grouping, surviving only as a soloist. Harmonies were tampered with. An ordinary chord (the triad that most soloists had been content with over the previous two decades) was embellished with a far greater range of added notes, including chromatic notes, and the passing harmonies – the 'changes', as jazz players often call them – grew more intricate. This meant that the ground-plan for improvisation, the map upon which the soloist relies, became at once more complex but also more stimulating. If there were increased difficulties there were also new possibilities. All the same, the pattern of the music remained as it was, most pieces still based on either the twelve-bar blues or the AABA form of the pop-song. An innovation was the way the musicians would take the harmonies of a better-than-average pop-song – *Indiana*, say or *Cherokee* – and expand them, adding passing chords and constructing what amounted to a brand-new theme, and one which often possessed such identity that it was given a fresh title. Good examples of this are *Groovin' High* (based on

57

Whispering), *Ornithology* (*How High The Moon*) and *Hot House* (*What Is This Thing Called Love*).

Chord sequence of 12 bar blues played by Bebop musicians in the mid 1940s

There will always be dispute about which musicians were really responsible for the innovations. With any dissident movement in the arts, however, there is always a general trend, a body of people working along similar lines, until eventually the new discoveries are summarized in the work of a single individual. At the end of the 1920s it was Louis Armstrong who stood as exemplar for the period. His counterpart in the 1940s was Charlie Parker, a musician of equal artistic stature and one who imposed his sound and phrasing upon his contemporaries every bit as completely as Armstrong had done fifteen or so years earlier. It is arguable that Coleman Hawkins and Lester Young had, in their various ways, anticipated some of Parker's rhythmic devices, notably his habit of breaking time up, of basing a solo on half-beats rather than those actually played by the rhythm section. But it was Parker who synthesized the technique within the context of his style, for it was where Parker placed a note, its rhythmic more than its pitch value, that remained the secret of his uniqueness, the thing his imitators could never get right. Another characteristic of Parker's style was the way the melodic line broke away from the accepted four-square pattern of earlier improvisers, introducing an element of apparent discontinuity, long and short phrases being fitted together in a way that seem, in retrospect, reminiscent of the call-and-response pattern which goes all the way back to African music.

This new kind of jazz was first called rebop, then bebop, and finally just bop. It seems likely that this was no more than an onomatopoeic way of describing the opening rhythmic figure of a particular tune; but Professor Maurice Crane has put forward an attractive suggestion that the name might derive from the Spanish expression 'Arriba!' or 'Riba!', meaning 'Up', a favourite cry of

Theme of Charlie Parker's 'Ornithology'

encouragement among Cuban musicians, many of whom were involved in the New York jazz scene of the 1940s. It took a while for the public to accept bebop. By 1945, however, both Parker and Dizzy Gillespie were working on 52nd Street, although when they went to California later that year they met with a harsh reception. But the way in which the bebop musicians stuck to their aesthetic convictions, unpopular as these were at first, was indicative of another change that had taken place, this time within the psychology of the performer. The young jazz player had begun to think of his music as art and of himself as an artist. The quality or even the nature of the music he created may not have been radically different from that of his predecessors; his standpoint undoubtedly was.

Yet if the American West Coast was grudging in its encouragement of the new jazz, it proved, by contrast, to be something of a haven for advocates of the old. It was in San Francisco in 1940 that a dance-band trumpeter, Lu Watters, formed his Yerba Buena Jazz Band, modelling its style and instrumentation upon King Oliver's Creole Jazz Band. Three hundred miles to the south, in Los Angeles, Kid Ory had been living in retirement, but in 1944 he got together a band of New Orleans veterans and began a second career at the age of 58. These events stemmed from a fascination with New Orleans jazz that had taken root among young white record collectors. It had been fore-shadowed in the late 1930s by the success of Muggsy Spanier's Ragtimers and the popularity of the music – more or less Dixieland jazz adapted for a big band – played by the Bob Crosby and Woody Herman orchestras. Now record companies started reissuing classic items by Armstrong and Morton and Oliver. Little magazines, propagating a fundamentalist, back-to-the-Delta aesthetic, began appearing, not only in the United States but in wartime England too.

The most potent rallying-point was Bunk Johnson, who claimed to have played second cornet to Buddy Bolden – and to have had the instrument knocked from his mouth whenever he blew a wrong note. Rediscovered at the age of 63, Johnson was brought to New York in 1945, together with a band of elderly New Orleans musicians that included the clarinettist George Lewis. Lewis had been working as a stevedore and playing for as little as 50 or 75 cents a night. His sweet, rococo style, ornamentation rather than improvisation, was to

Top right: The Charlie Parker Band at Spotlite Club,
52nd Street, 1947 (Miles Davis is the trumpet player)
Bottom right: The Kid Ory Band

Left: Bunk Johnson
Above: Humphrey Lyttelton

become the most obsessive influence upon the many European bands which set out to recreate New Orleans jazz in the post-war years. Most of these used a banjo in the rhythm section, and the front-line players – depending on their allegiance – modelled themselves upon either King Oliver, Johnny Dodds and Kid Ory, or else Bunk Johnson, George Lewis and Jim Robinson. At first the audiences sat and listened respectfully; later on, Graeme Bell's Australian band, making an extended visit to London, showed that it was practical for New Orleans jazz to be danced to. British musicians who played a vital part in the revival included George Webb, Humphrey Lyttelton, Ken Colyer, Sandy Brown and Chris Barber. It was Barber's band which broke through to the wider public and led up to the situation at the start of the 1960s, when 'traditional' jazz enjoyed something of the popularity – and eventually lapsed into the same decline – that 'Swing' had done twenty years earlier.

It is significant that the New Orleans revival was almost entirely the work of elderly veterans or young white musicians. (None of the young Negro players showed any interest in the movement.) A good deal of the music they made was second-rate and imitative, and there was, for a time, a polarizing of jazz enthusiasts into supporters of 'traditional' and 'modern'. Yet the revival enabled a musician like Sidney Bechet to go on working and recording, receiving in his lifetime some of the acclaim that was denied to King Oliver, Johnny Dodds, Tommy Ladnier and other fine musicians who died while New Orleans jazz was still sorely out of fashion. Most important of all, jazz had been given perspective, the past rescued, the history put right.

MODERN JAZZ

All major jazz innovations have been started by soloists. It seems to be later on, during the period of consolidation, that composers develop an orchestral counterpart. It was the same with bebop. Tadd Dameron and Thelonious Monk were among the first off the mark, writing themes for small groups, while Dizzy Gillespie formed a big band which played aggressively up-to-date scores by Gil Fuller and George Russell. Ironically enough, it was a white group, the Woody Herman orchestra, that achieved commercial success with a blend of the new and the not-quite-so-new, of bebop solos inside what was still, despite the fresh harmonic trappings, a swing-band setting. But it was a nine-piece group which Miles Davis assembled in the autumn of 1948, which played in public for no more than a fortnight yet managed to get recorded, that had the most lasting influence. By the standards of the time its instrumentation was unorthodox: trumpet, trombone, French horn, alto and baritone saxes, piano, bass and drums. At the hands of Gil Evans, Gerry Mulligan and John Lewis, all of whom wrote for the band, this grouping produced the most interesting textures since the orchestras of Duke Ellington and Don Redman. The music also typified a shift that was taking place, from declamation to under-statement, from directness to implication, from – to drop into the terminology of the period – 'hot' to 'cool'. Nevertheless, it would be false to imagine that the Miles Davis Band, all on its own, inaugurated this new trend. There was, for one thing, the pianist Lennie Tristano, who in partnership with the alto saxophonist, Lee Konitz, had made a number of icily perfect records. But the true begetter was a man of the swing era, Lester Young. Even in the 1930s, Young's style was oblique, detached, and he would concentrate upon such subtleties as using alternative fingerings to obtain different densities of sound from the same note. Yet it was not Young himself who was to show the way but those tenor players who had adapted his style, notably the white saxophonist Stan Getz.

Geography and economics were now playing a much smaller role in shaping the history of jazz. Aesthetic and technical curiosity had largely taken over as the sources of change. Yet it is intriguing that even as late as the 1950s a geographical area, the West Coast, should

Miles Davis

have given its name to a school of jazz. The movement centred around Los Angeles, a city to which many musicians migrated during and and just after World War II, mainly because of the quantity of work that was available in film, radio, TV and recording studios. The vast majority of these musicians were white, for Negroes were discriminated against in these fields, and because West Coast jazz was predominantly white music it is easy to draw a parallel with events in New York at the end of the 1920s. There was the same emphasis upon technical perfection and purity of tone, a priority given to precision rather than intensity. There was even a rejection of the personal timbres, a move towards the standardised sound of the concert or session player. Instruments such as the flute, oboe, cello and French horn, rarely employed in jazz before, became almost commonplace. The European tradition was raided, with John Lewis as just one of a number of jazz composers who attempted to make use of such classical devices as fugue and canon. Quite a few of these West Coast musicians worked in the various orchestras led by Stan Kenton, a bandleader who symbolized another of the ways in which jazz was striving for respectability. When Kenton wanted it to, his band could swing in an exciting, highly traditional way, but there were also occasions when Kenton featured compositions in a pseudo-classical idiom, attempts at a rapprochement between jazz and concert music that were to be continued by others under the label of 'Third Stream Music'. Two of the most successful small groups of the 1950s also came from the West Coast, one led by the baritone saxophonist Gerry Mulligan, the other by the pianist Dave Brubeck. The latter will probably be remembered for introducing time-signatures – $\frac{5}{4}$, $\frac{11}{4}$, – that were new to jazz, and for interesting large number of young people in the music. The essence of Mulligan's jazz was the constant interplay of ideas between the two front-line players in his Quartet. This revival of collective improvisation was also to be found in the work of the Modern Jazz Quartet – from the East Coast, this time – an all-percussion group (vibraphone, piano, bass, drums) led by John Lewis.

The 1950s were very much years of retrenchment, of consolidation, yet before the decade was over a reaction had set in against 'cool' jazz. It was represented at one edge by an attempt to reach back into history, to make use of Negro folk-roots, and at the other by a

deliberate breaking away from accepted patterns and discipline. Negro musicians of the 1930s and 1940s had tended to be scornful of the past, rejecting Oliver and Morton as crude, even laughable, feeling wary about identifying with the earlier forms of jazz and blues, not only from a lack of sympathy but also because these idioms seemed to stretch halfway back to slavery, a reminder of humiliation. It was one of the penalties jazz paid for being an enclave of show business; nothing obscures an historical viewpoint so much as a need to follow the newest fashion. But the generation of Negroes that grew up in the 1950s was aware of a sense of cultural identity. Where their fathers had straightened out the kinks in their hair and accepted the values of white American society, these men took pride in their blackness and African ancestry. Gospel music and the blues had been present in Negro society all the time, but now gospel phrases and rhythms (especially the use of triple time) cropped up in the music of groups like those led by the pianist Horace Silver and the drummer Art Blakey. Negro popular music also reflected this reappraisal, even achieving – in 'soul' music, and especially in the singing of Ray Charles – a fusion of blues and gospel. But perhaps the most successful synthesizing of these elements – artistically, anyway – was carried out by Charles Mingus, a virtuoso bassist and one of the most original jazz composers. Mingus also harnessed the talents of younger musicians – the alto saxophonist Eric Dolphy, for example – who were moving away from set patterns of improvising. And in his bands the practice of collective improvisation embraced the bass and drums, so that the terms 'front-line' and 'rhythm section' ceased to carry their traditional meanings.

If Mingus is one man whose work has very obviously influenced the jazz of the 1960s, another is Miles Davis. Not only has Davis continued, right up to the present, to develop new methods of solo-playing, he also collaborated with the orchestrator, Gil Evans, in a unique set of concertos featuring himself on the fluegel-horn, an instrument he popularised in jazz, and his Quintet played a major part in shifting improvisation away from standard chord progressions, using scales instead. A member of the Davis Quintet at that time was the tenor saxophonist John Coltrane, who went on to develop this

Top left: Stan Kenton and his orchestra in London, 1956
Bottom left: Gerry Mulligan Quartet (Bob Brookmeyer is on valve trombone)

Extract from Ornette Coleman's solo in 'Ramblin'

technique. Indeed, Coltrane's habit of simplifying the chord structure, then using the scales and extensions suggested by this, became one of the basic approaches of the new school of musicians. Ornette Coleman, on the other hand, ignored chords altogether and began playing free melodic lines on his alto saxophone. But not entirely free, for his solos normally relate to a starting-note or a centre of tonality, he sticks to a steady pulse, and his music rarely fails to swing. Of the so-called avant-garde performers, it is Ornette Coleman who has probably created the most striking and valuable music so far.

71

Top left: Ornette Coleman
Bottom left: Eric Dolphy

Other contributions have been made by the pianist Cecil Taylor and a large body of young, iconoclastic players, ranging from Archie Shepp, a saxophonist whose style has obvious affinities with that of Coleman Hawkins, to Albert Ayler, who makes use of sound rather than pitched notes. It is still too early to judge the stature of most of these performers or to see where they are taking jazz. One thing is certain. Even though a few of the new musicians have links with the Black Power movement and view their work – Black Music, they insist, not jazz – as an expression of the new social and political forces at work in black communities, this music does not enjoy the popularity with the Negro public that earlier forms of jazz have done. Just like the work of white avant-garde players, it is an aesthetic experiment, experienced and enjoyed – unlike the Negro jazz of the 1920s and 1930s, unlike such present day Negro favourites as James Brown, B. B. King and Lou Rawls – only by a minority audience.

73

Top left: Duke Ellington and John Coltrane
Bottom left: Modern Jazz Quartet
Above: Sun Ra and his Solar Arkestra

AN INTERNATIONAL MUSIC

Jazz stopped being an exclusively Negro music sometime before World War I. It ceased to be purely American somewhere in the 1920s or 1930s, after Sidney Bechet had been to Odessa and Kharkov and played with Tommy Ladnier in Moscow, before the curtains went up on Duke Ellington's band at the London Palladium in 1933. But the trouble about learning to play jazz outside America was that the musician lacked a tradition close at hand, a community of performers he could work and compete with. He had to rely instead upon hearing the occasional visiting American and listening to his gramophone records. That is how Europe's first original jazz musician, the guitarist Django Reinhardt, developed his style. That this style turned out to be a hybrid, a sort of gypsy jazz, the blues-playing closer to the Mediterranean than the Mississippi Delta, was natural and in its way quite proper. And the Quintet of the Hot Club of France, which Reinhardt led with the violinist Stephane Grappelly, had an instrumentation – violin, three guitars, bass – that seemed wildly improbable by contemporary American standards. But France was in the vanguard of European jazz quite early on. It was there, after all, in 1934 that Hugues Panassié's 'Hot Jazz', the first book of jazz criticism, was published. The growth of jazz in Britain was complicated by the fact that from 1936 until 1956 a deadlock existed between the Musicians' Union and the American Federation of Musicians, which prevented Americans from performing in Britain and Britons from working in the United States. Yet British jazz already had a talented composer in Spike Hughes, even if he gave up early, and by the end of the 1930s its first major soloist, the Scottish trombone player, George Chisholm.

Not until after the war did Europe produce more than a handful of jazz musicians – and the rhythm sections were still stiff and unyielding. For a time 'traditional' jazz spread everywhere. Indeed, it seemed to take the place of folk music in those urban, industrialized countries – Britain, France, Belgium, Holland – where local traditions were weak. (It was noticeable that jazz did not make the same inroads in Spain, Italy and other predominantly agrarian nations where folk traditions were still alive.) Once jazz began to be performed, the creation of a valid tradition was only a matter of time. In Britain it resulted in

Top right: Django Reinhardt with the quintet of the
Hot Club of France
Bottom right: John Surman

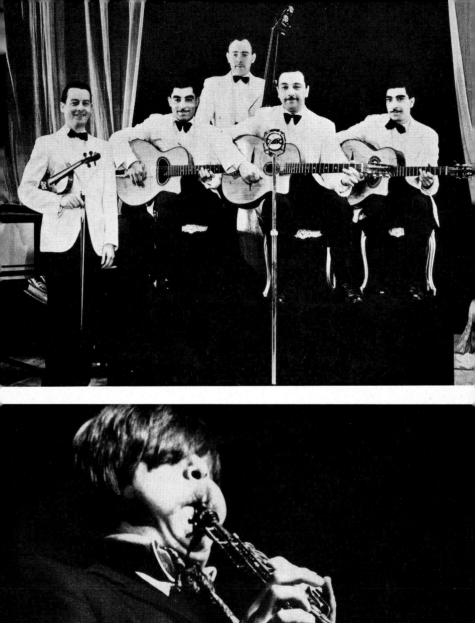

a number of gifted individuals, among them the vibraphonist Victor Feldman, the clarinettist Sandy Brown, and the drummer Phil Seamen, but not until the 1960s was there an upsurge of gifted players in any quantity. It could now be argued that the British baritone saxophonist John Surman is equal, if not superior, to any American, while the fact that in 1968 Miles Davis chose a British bassist, Dave Holland, to work in his Quintet is another indication of the progress that has been made. This improvement is partly due to the social acceptance of jazz as a music which it was natural for a European to play, partly a result of the increased opportunities for working alongside Americans. It is a situation that has prevailed for much longer on the other side of the English Channel. Indeed, the migration of Americans to Europe, principally to France, started in the 1920s. Most of those were Negro musicians who found living conditions more tolerable, but during the last decade there has been a large influx of players who find it easier to get work in Europe than in America.

But the traffic of ideas is not confined to these two continents. The growing awareness in the West of the values of Oriental music has been reflected in jazz. For a start, the methods of musicians like John Coltrane have similarities with the way an Indian performer improvises on a raga. Coltrane himself consciously leant upon Indian patterns in some of his later recordings, even getting his bassist to supply a drone and his drummer to build a network of cross-rhythms. Jazz, in fact, has been influenced by Oriental structures, rhythms and procedures, while pop music, which patronised Indian music for a short time in the 1960s, took only the wiry twang of the sitar. Of the several head-on attempts at fusing Indian music with jazz, the most successful has been the work of a double quartet of Indian players and jazz musicians, led respectively by the Indian violinist and composer, John Mayer, and the West Indian alto saxophonist, Joe Harriott.

The link with the Orient is a recent one, but that with Africa is the oldest of all. Yet, perhaps because so many African elements already exist inside jazz, there has been surprisingly little exchanging of ideas. The influence upon jazz has usually been second-hand, through Cuban or other Caribbean rhythms, although the new awareness of African ancestry has inspired a number of black Americans, most of them drummers, to attempt pastiches or adaptations of African music. The

76

Top right: Chris McGregor's Blue Notes
Bottom right: Don Cherry

impact of jazz upon Africa can be found in the 'high-life' music of West Africa and the *kwela* bands in the cities of South Africa. Indeed, South Africa has produced a number of good jazz musicians, including the alto saxophonists Kiepie Moeketsi and Dudu Pukwana, and the pianist-composers Dollar Brand and Chris McGregor. (McGregor now leads an all-African band – white as well as black – in London.) Typical of South African jazz are the riffs and sweet, fat chords of *kwela*, and the over-riding sound of saxophones, an imbalance explained by the fact that most of the musicians start by blowing penny whistles as children and simply move on to alto saxophones as they grow up.

But the most obvious bartering of ideas has been with the music of Latin America and the Caribbean islands, music that itself stems from the same racial mixtures as jazz, the fusion of African slave traditions with European – in this case French and Spanish, rather than Anglo-Saxon – forms and harmonies. This blending cropped up in the music of the New Orleans Creoles. And although the Cuban influence is generally associated with modern jazz, it actually began earlier; Duke Ellington recorded a jazz rumba, *Maori*, in 1931. But it was the young musicians of the 1940s – notably Dizzy Gillespie with his big band, and later on the Stan Kenton orchestra – who brought in Cuban drummers and tried to expand the rhythmic basis of jazz. The most recent attempt at fusing jazz with South American music was the development of the bossa nova, a combination of the melodic lines of modern jazz and the rhythm of the Brazilian samba.

Cultural exchanges are not just a matter of geography, of exotic transplants. For a large part of its history, jazz has been conscious of a subordinate relationship with European music. It was this sense of cultural inferiority, as illusory as it is pathetic, that caused even musicians as distinguished as Duke Ellington and Charlie Parker to look on working with a string ensemble as a status symbol, a mark of acceptance. Although George Gershwin's *Rhapsody In Blue* was not jazz in a strict sense, it typified this urge to make jazz respectable, a motive that underlies a good deal of 'Third Stream Music'. And composers continue trying to integrate jazz in the structural apparatus of European music; use has even been made of the twelve-tone serial technique, both loosely, by Don Ellis and John Carisi, and strictly, in a set of compositions by the Scottish musician David Mack. The crucial relationship, however, is that between jazz and pop music. In the past jazz has taken pop-songs as material for improvisation, and in its turn jazz has been drawn upon as a source of commercial techniques. (The music of the Glenn Miller Orchestra of the 1940s was very largely a formalising of Duke Ellington's repertoire of sounds, even the scoring of clarinet in with brass, while the twelve-bar blues has been the basis of a vast amount of recent pop music, beginning with the early work of the Beatles.) Jazz has suffered through the shift in dancing habits, for jazz is no longer in direct touch with the youngest section of the public, as it was even as late as the early 1960s. This has meant a retreat – in America as well as Britain – from some areas where jazz has been used for dancing, and fewer opportunities for jazz players to work in clubs. All of which would indicate that the future for jazz lies in its status as art music. Or at least that seems to be the situation until one takes into account the most recent developments in pop music itself. What is happening there seems strangely akin with what happened in jazz, the separation of more ambitious elements – musicians intent upon using the medium expressively, upon communicating more than basic emotions – from the functional setting. It has led to the creation of a species of pop music – 'intellectual pop', 'progressive pop', the names are still being bandied about – with aesthetic rather than purely commercial or functional aims. Groups like The Cream, the Mothers of Invention and the Jefferson Airplane include musicians who have either come up through jazz or else have begun to improvise within the conventions of pop music. The fact that the sound – electronic instruments rather than the traditional brass and reeds – is very different from jazz seems unimportant. The situation is still one of ferment, but at least there is the possibility of a metamorphosis, of jazz moving ahead and yet managing to preserve its common touch.

BIBLIOGRAPHY
AND DISCOGRAPHY

History and Criticism

DANKWORTH, A. *Jazz: an introduction to its musical basis* O.U.P., 1968. 16s.

Short – 90 pp. – but useful guide to the musicological background.

HENTOFF, N. AND MCCARTHY, A., eds. *Jazz* Cassell, 1960. o.p.

Essays on various topics, including ragtime, boogie-woogie, Kansas City and Charlie Parker.

HODEIR, A. *Jazz: its evolution and essence* Secker & Warburg, 1956. o.p.; Trans-Atlantic Book Service, 4s.

Valuable analyses of jazz from 1930 onwards but erratic on earlier periods.

NEWTON, F. *The jazz scene* MacGibbon & Kee, 1959. o.p.; Penguin Books, 1961. 4s.

Good all-round coverage of economic background as well as of musicians.

SCHULLER, G. *Early jazz* O.U.P., 1968. 55s.

Covers jazz history up to 1931; the best musicological study so far.

STEARNS, M. *The story of jazz* Sidgwick & Jackson, 1957. o.p.; New English Library, 1968. 7s. 6d.

Excellent general history.

Social and Economic Background

CONDON, E. *We called it music* P. Davies, 1948, o.p.; Transworld, 2nd edn. 1962. paperback o.p.

Racy but illuminating autobiography by this white Chicago guitarist.

HENTOFF, N. *The jazz life* P. Davies, 1962. o.p.; Hamilton, 1964. Panther paperback. o.p.

Describes – and often criticises – the world of the jazz musician.

SHAPIRO, N. AND HENTOFF, N., eds. *Hear me talkin' to ya* P. Davies, 1955. o.p.; Penguin Books, 1962. 6s.

The history of jazz in the words of the musicians themselves.

LOMAX, A. *Mister Jelly Roll* Cassell, 1952. o.p.

Romantic but enlightening study of the life and times of Jelly Roll Morton.

Left: Don Ellis with amplified trumpet

OLIVER, P. *Conversation with the blues* Cassell, 1965. 36s.
Interviews with American blues performers.

SMITH, Willie 'The Lion'. *Music on my mind* MacGibbon & Kee, 1965. 30s.
Colourful autobiography of one of the best Harlem pianists; full of information about jazz in New York during the 1920s and 1930s.

SPELLMAN, A. B. *Four lives in the bebop business* MacGibbon & Kee, 1967. 36s.
Studies of Ornette Coleman, Jackie McLean, Herbie Nichols and Cecil Taylor.

---

1. THE BEGINNINGS

Negro Folk Music of Africa and America Folkways 4500 (2 LPs)
'*Southern Folk Heritage Series.*' Field recordings made by Alan Lomax.
  '*Sounds of the South*' Atlantic 590 033
  (This volume includes spirituals and ballads.)
  Negro Church Music Atlantic 590 029
  '*Roots of The Blues*' Atlantic 590 019
  (Contains field hollers, work songs and primitive blues.)
  '*Blues Roll On*' Atlantic 590 025 (Country blues.)
'*Conversation With The Blues.*' Field recordings made by Paul Oliver. Decca LK4664
(Includes interviews with a number of blues musicians.)
'*Out Came The Blues*' Vol. 1: Ace of Hearts AH72, Vol. 2: Ace of Hearts AH158
(Valuable anthology of country and city blues by professional blues singers and musicians.)
Bessie Smith: '*The Bessie Smith Story*' Vols. 1-4,
CBS BPG62377080
'*The Golden Age of Ragtime*' Riverside RLP 12-110
(No longer available but worth searching for. Transcriptions from early piano rolls of compositions by Scott Joplin and other ragtime composers.)
Young Tuxedo Brass Band: '*New Orlean Joys*' Atlantic 590 023
(Latterday recording of a New Orleans street band.)

2. NEW ORLEANS

'*The Sound of New Orleans*' Vols. 1-3, CBS BPG 62232-4
(No longer available but worth searching for. This anthology contains examples of both white and Negro New Orleans bands, including many obscure groups.)
'*Original Dixieland Jazz Band*' RCA RD 7919
(Includes original 1917 recordings.)
'*Music of New Orleans*'
Vol. 1: Music of the Streets and of Mardi Gras Topic 12T53
Vol. 3: Music Of The Dance Halls Topic 12T55
(Recordings made in the early 1950s and of great documentary interest.)
'*New Orleans Today*' Vol. 1: 77 LA12/16, Vol. 2: 77 LA 12/29
(More recent recordings. The bands include those of Kid Thomas, Kid Howard and Peter Bocage.)
'*New Orleans Jazz*' Brunswick LAT8146
(1940 recordings by famous New Orleans musicians: Louis Armstrong, Sidney Bechet, Johnny Dodds, Jimmy Noone, Henry 'Red' Allen and Zutty Singleton.)
Sidney Bechet: '*Bechet of New Orleans*' RCA RD7696
(Mostly recordings made in the 1940s, by one of the great New Orleans reed players.)
Records by *Bunk Johnson, George Lewis* and *Kid Ory* will be found in Section 6.

3. CHICAGO AND KANSAS CITY

Louis Armstrong: '*His Greatest Years*'
   Vol. 1: Parlophone PMC1140   Vol. 3: Parlophone PMC1146
   Vol. 2: Parlophone PMC1142   Vol. 4: Parlophone PMC1150
Bix Beiderbecke with Frankie Trumbauer's Orchestra: '*Bix and Tram, 1927*' Parlophone PMC7064
Jelly Roll Morton: '*The King of New Orleans Jazz*' RCA RD27113
Bennie Moten and his Kansas City Orchestra: '*K.C. Jazz*' RCA RD7660
(Recordings made between 1926 and 1929. The slightly later, and best, recordings have not been issued in Britain but are available on

American RCA LPV514.)
King Oliver's Creole Jazz Band: Parlophone PMC7032
(Pre-electric 1923 recordings.)
Joe Turner with Pete Johnson's Orchestra: 'Jumpin The Blues'
Fontana 688 802ZL
(Recorded in 1948 but typical of Kansas City blues singing and small
band work.)
Jimmy and Mama Yancey: 'Low Down Dirty Blues' Atlantic
590 018

4. NEW YORK

Duke Ellington and his Orchestra: 'The Ellington Era, Vol. 2 –
1927/40' CBS BPG66302 (3 LPs)
Fletcher Henderson and his Connie's Inn Orchestra: 'Smack'
Ace of Hearts AH41
James P. Johnson: Transatlantic XTRA 1024
(Piano solos by the greatest of the Harlem pianists.)
Eddie Lang – Lonnie Johnson: 'Blue Guitars' Parlophone
PMC7019
(The two most brilliant guitarists of the 1920s, one an Italian-
American session-man, the other a Negro blues player.)
Red Nichols and his Five Pennies: Ace of Hearts AH63
(New York white jazz of the 1920s.)
Don Redman: CBS 52539
(Redman was Fletcher Henderson's chief arranger in the 1920s;
he started up his own orchestra in 1931.)
Luis Russell: 'The Luis Russell Story' Parlophone PMC7025
(A New York big band full of New Orleans sidemen – Henry 'Red'
Allen, Albert Nicholas, Pops Foster, Paul Barbarin etc.
Willie 'The Lion' Smith/Luckey Roberts: 'Luckey and the Lion'
Good Time Jazz LAG12256
(Recorded in 1958 but nevertheless authentic performances by two of
the leading Harlem pianists of the 1920s.)
Chick Webb: 'Midnite In Harlem' Ace of Hearts AH32
(Resident band at the Savoy Ballroom for many years.)
'The Original Sound of the 20s' CBS BPG62545/6/7 (3 LPs)
(An anthology of pop music and jazz of the 1920s.)

5. SWING
'*Spirituals to Swing Concerts*' Fontana FJL 401 & 402
(Recorded at Carnegie Hall in 1938 and 1939. Performers include
Benny Goodman Sextet, Count Basie orchestra, Lester Young,
James P. Johnson, Sidney Bechet, Golden Gate Quartet, Joe Turner
and Ida Cox.)
Count Basie and his Orchestra: Brunswick LAT8028 or Ace of
Hearts AH111.
(The original, pre-war Count Basie band. Both LPs are good, with
some titles in common.)
Charlie Christian: '*Solo Flight, Vol. 1*' CBS BPG62581
(Christian playing with various Benny Goodman groups, notably
the Sextet.)
Duke Ellington and His Orchestra: '*At His Very Best*' RCA RD27133
(The Ellington band of 1940, with Jimmy Blanton on bass.)
Benny Goodman: '*Carnegie Hall Concert*' CBS BPG66202 (2 LPs)
Lionel Hampton: '*Jivin' The Vibes*' Camden CDN129
(Hampton leading small pick-up groups.)
Coleman Hawkins: '*Swing*' Fontana FJL102.
Billie Holiday: '*The Golden Years, Vol. 2*' CBS BPG66301 (3 LPs)
(Recordings made between 1935 and 1942, including several with
Lester Young.)
Jimmie Lunceford Orchestra: '*Lunceford Special*' CBS 52567
Art Tatum: '*Here's Art Tatum*' Ace of Hearts AH109
Fats Waller: '*Fats 1935-37*' RCA RD27047
Lester Young: '*Lester Leaps Again*' Fontana FJL128
(Includes alternative 'takes' of the same titles, with Young taking
different solos.)
'*The Glenn Miller Years*' 6 LP set issued by Readers' Digest
(The most comprehensive collection of recordings by big bands of
the swing era, including many commercial dance orchestras. Not all
jazz but a remarkable cross-section of the period.) RDM 2171-6

6. BEBOPPERS AND REVIVALISTS
'*The Bebop Era*' RCA RD7909
(Anthology of mid-1940s recordings by Dizzy Gillespie, Charlie

Parker, Fats Navarro, Kenny Clarke, etc.)
Dizzy Gillespie – Thelonious Monk – Charlie Christian. Society SOC996
(Recordings made at Minton's Playhouse in 1940.)
Dizzy Gillespie: RCA RD7827
(Big band and small group recordings from the mid-1940s.)
Thelonious Monk: 'Vol. 1' Blue Note BLP1510
(Includes original recordings of *Round Midnight, Epistrophy,* etc.)
Charlie Parker: 'The Pick of Parker' Verve VLP9078
Charlie Parker: 'Vol. 4: Jazz At Massey Hall' Saga Eros 8031
(Recording of concert in Toronto in 1953 with Gillespie, Parker, Bud Powell, Charles Mingus and Max Roach.)
Bud Powell: 'The Vintage Years' Verve VLP9075
Muggsy Spanier's Ragtime Band: 'The Great 16' RCA RD27132
Lu Watters/Bunk Johnson: 'Bunk and Lu' Good Time Jazz LAG12121
Kid Ory's Creole Jazz Band: Good Time Jazz LAG12104
Bunk Johnson and his Superior Jazz Band: Good Time Jazz LAG545
(Includes Bunk Johnson talking about his early life in New Orleans.)
George Lewis and his New Orleans Stompers: Vocalion LAE12005
Ken Colyer's Jazzmen: 'New Orleans in London' Decca LF1152
(One of the first – and best – British revivalist bands.)

7. MODERN JAZZ

Dave Brubeck Quartet: 'Jazz At Oberlin' Ace of Hearts AH167
Ornette Coleman: 'The Shape Of Jazz To Come' Atlantic (M) 587022, (S) 588022
John Coltrane: 'A Love Supreme' HMV (M) CLP1869, (S) CSD3547
Miles Davis: 'Birth of the Cool' Capitol T1974
(The 1948/9 recordings by Davis's nine-piece band.)
Miles Davis: 'Miles Ahead' CBS BPG/SBPG 62496
(Collaborations with the orchestrator Gil Evans.)
Miles Davis: 'Kind of Blue' CBS BPG/SBPG 62066
(1959 Sextet recordings with Cannonball Adderley, John Coltrane and Bill Evans.)
Stan Getz: 'The Getz Age' Columbia 33SX1707
(Getz Quartet recordings of 1950-2.)
Stan Kenton: 'The Great Big Bands, Vol. 4' Capitol T20841

(Recordings made between 1950 and 1956.)
Lee Konitz/Lennie Tristano: 'Subconscious Lee' Transatlantic
XTRA 5049
Charles Mingus: 'Mingus Dynasty' CBS BPG/SBPG 62261
Modern Jazz Quartet: 'Concorde' Transatlantic PR7005
Gerry Mulligan: 'The Original Gerry Mulligan Quartet' Fontana
688 121 ZL
Sonny Rollins – Clifford Brown – Max Roach: 'Three Giants'
Transatlantic PR7291

8. AN INTERNATIONAL MUSIC

*Django Reinhardt, Stephane Grappelly and the Quintet of the Hot
Club of France* Ace of Clubs ACL1158
'Scrapbook of British Jazz' Ace of Clubs ACL1105
(Ranges from the late 1920s – Fred Elizalde – up to post-war tra-
ditional jazz, including tracks by Spike Hughes, Nat Gonella, George
Chisholm and Chris Barber.)
Stan Tracey Quartet: 'Jazz Suite' Columbia SX1774
(One of the most successful modern British records; Tracey's suite is
based on Dylan Thomas's verse-play 'Under Milk Wood'.)
Zbigniew Namyslowski Modern Jazz Quartet: 'Lola' Decca LK 4644
(A modern Polish jazz group making use of Polish folk themes.)
Zagreb Jazz Quartet: 'With Pain I Was Born' Fontana FJL900
(One of the best Yugoslav jazz groups.)
Chris McGregor Group: 'Very Urgent' Polydor 184137
(All-African sextet in London playing *kwela*-influenced avant-garde
jazz.)
Joe Harriott – John Mayer Double Quintet: 'Indo-Jazz Fusions'
Columbia (M) SX/(S) SCX 6122
(Indian and jazz musicians working together.)
Dizzy Gillespie and his Orchestra. Pye-Vogue VRL3011
(Recorded in Paris in 1948 by a band including the Cuban drummer
Chano Pozo.)
Bud Shank/Laurindo Almeida: 'Jazz Goes Brazil' Fontana
688 001 ZL
(An early example of jazz musicians using Brazilian themes and
rhythms.)

Jazz Abstractions' Atlantic 587043
(Compositions by Gunther Schuller and Jim Hall, performed by
Ornette Coleman, Eric Dolphy, Bill Evans, Jim Hall and The Con-
temporary String Quartet.)
Don Ellis Orchestra: *'Electric Bath'* CBS (M & S) 63230.
(Big band making use of electronic devices, including a loop delay
echo chamber, as well as complex time signatures, eclectic but
interesting.)
Gary Burton Quartet: 'Lofty Fake Anagram' RCA SF/RD7923
(A modern jazz group which incorporates, especially in the guitar
playing, some elements of present-day pop music.)

ACKNOWLEDGEMENTS

Acknowledgement is due to the following for permission to reproduce illustrations:
PHILIPPE GRAS), Don Cherry, page 77; JAZZ JOURNAL Preservation Jazz Band, page 27,
Original Dixieland Jazz Band, page 28, Tony Jackson, page 29, Bix Beiderbecke, page
31, Sunset Café site (photo, Chuck Sengstock), page 39, Henry 'Red' Allen, page 46,
'Fats' Waller, page 48, Thelonious Monk, page 55, Kid Ory Band (photo, Ray Avery),
page 61, Duke Ellington (photo, Bob Chiraldini), page 72; JAZZ MONTHLY Ma Rainey,
page 16, record label, page 17, Albert Ammons (photo, Otto Hess), page 35, Dizzy
Gillespie (photo, Ken Palmer), page 56, Eric Dolphy (photo, Bill Wagg), page 70;
MAX JONES New Orleans band, page 26, James P. Johnson, page 41, Jimmie
Lunceford Orchestra, page 50, Bunk Johnson, page 62, Quintet of Hot Club
of France, page 75; MELODY MAKER Gerry Mulligan, page 68, John Surman, page 75;
PAUL OLIVER Lightnin' Hopkins, page 20; PHOTO FILES King Oliver, page 35, Bennie
Moten Orchestra, page 37, Duke Ellington Band, page 43, Benny Goodman Orchestra,
page 48, Count Basie Orchestra, page 50, Coleman Hawkins Band, page 52, Charlie
Parker Band, page 61; POPPERFOTO African drummers, page 13; RADIO TIMES
HULTON PICTURE LIBRARY slave ship, bill of sale, page 15, cotton picking, page 16,
drawing of New Orleans, New Orleans street, page 24, Louis Armstrong, page 31,
Cotton Club, page 43, Lionel Hampton, page 52, Humphrey Lyttelton, page 63,
Stan Kenton Orchestra, page 68; DAVID REDFERN PHOTOGRAPHY Modern Jazz Quartet,
page 72, Don Ellis, page 80; VALERIE WILMER Miles Davis, page 66, Ornette Coleman,
page 70, Sun Ra, Boykins & Allen, page 73, Chris McGregor's Blue Notes, page 77.

Acknowledgement is due to the following for permission to reprint musical extracts:—
HERMAN DAREWSKI MUSIC PUBLISHING CO. for *Maple Leaf Rag* by Scott Joplin;
B. FELDMAN & CO. LTD for *West End Blues* by Joe Oliver and Clarence Williams;
KENSINGTON MUSIC LTD for *Ramblin* by Ornette Coleman; J. R. LAFLEUR & SON LTD
for *A Sm-o-o-oth One* by Bennie Goodman; LORNA MUSIC CO. LTD for *Ornithology* by
Bennie Harris and Charlie Parker (Copyright for the World by Criterion Music
Corporation of Hollywood); PETER MAURICE MUSIC CO. LTD for *Honky Tonk Train
Blues* by Meade Lux Lewis; ROBBINS MUSIC CORPORATION LTD for *Panama* by W. H.
Tylers (Copyright Leo Feist Inc., New York); SOUTHERN MUSIC PUBLISHING CO.
LTD for *Toby* by Bennie Moten.